The B

CW00435540

Muskaan Nahar

BookLeaf
Publishing

Presentation by *BookLeaf Publishing*

Web: www.bookleafpub.com

E-mail: info@bookleafpub.com

ISBN: 9789357440608

First edition 2023

This book is dedicted to all the souls discovering and growing into the best version of themselves. And to the little girl who dreamed of this.

ACKNOWLEDGEMENT

I want to thank my family of eight, who gave me the passion for literature in the first place and supported me for anything and everything in life.

I specially want to thank my sister, for being the reason of everything I believed in and everything I want to be.

I want to thank my small but amazing group of Stratford road, UK, who have been like a family far away from home, and took care of me in every way possible.

Last but not the least, I would like to thank BookLeaf Publishing for providing me with this opportunity and resources to fulfill a life-long dream.

Family

It is a strange word
A stranger bond
It goes far beyond its meaning
And further beyond its cause

They make you grow
They make you love
They give you the world
And won't let you hurt

They aren't superheroes
Sometimes a mess
They are still healing
And learning to express

They taught you hurt
Even if it was unknown
But their love overpowers
Everything you've ever known

No matter how broken
No matter how bruised
It is still never ending
And mends up as new

You are miles apart
Or you are right there
No amount of time together
Could ever be fair

Some strange minds
But stranger hearts
But at the end of it all
Your family is your part…!

A Heart's Desire

Watch the fire
Stand the heat,
Of who do I listen
Of what do I speak...

The more the oblivious
The less I can be,
As life and light
Don't let me be...

The heart at one
The mind at two,
I see them gone
When I'm black and blue...

The noise around
The silence within,
Pulls me apart
As so bloody keen...

The soft thread now
Has turned into a wire,
To hold on tight
To a heart's desire...!

Love Tonight

Your arms feel me
Beyond skin and bones
As if you are cuddling my soul,

Your lips are so
Like a forbidden fruit
And the taste takes on a toll,

I'm on the sweetest high
With the burn of your touch
And you consume me whole,

No fears or regrets
The moments of passion shared
As your mark became a mole,

Give me the wild delight
As I gain your love tonight
While now, we never let go...

Melody

The uncertain phase of life
where the heart tunes up
with something you long for,
And yet your voice wants
to hum the unsung melody.

No parting words, no whisper made
A wave of questions with a restless strain
with a lot of strength,
sung the melody again!

Just Me

I'm in a crowd
Chatters and buzzes
Everyone talking to everyone
Yet there is an undisputed silence
Within me...
Just within me...

I hope to jump out
Cross all about
I try to fly high above the cry
Yet there is a lack of flight
Within me...
Just within me...

I'm goint to let things happen
As long as I can
Going to hope for one more day
To let in the smile and glory
Within me...
Just within me...

I Belong

Love me to show how much you care,
Love me to make others beware...

Hold me all through the day,
Hold me all through the night...

Kiss me gently with your soft lips,
Kiss me while I embrace your hips...

Comfort me while I'm in your arms,
Comfort me with your charm...

Tell me you will always be mine,
Tell me I am your shrine...

I feel the need within,
Because I love you...
With all my heart,
I belong to you...!

Running Away

The dearth of wind around sways
Making me drop down to weight
The madness of the wind plays
Pushing on to finish the way
Can't keep running away...

The color in the sky burns away
My faith in life goes astray
The ashes of the moment fly away
There is still something everyday
Can't keep running away...

Walking over an array
Resting at the edge of the bay
Thinking of everything obeyed
Looking for a reason to stay
Can't keep running away...

The heart's fire turned gray
Left with unpleasant pieces to convey
To embark the moulding today
The hopes within all ricochet
It is time to run away...

Peace

Clouds that fly above the sky...
Wishes that linger upon our eyes...
I like to hold onto these...
That is where I find my peace!

Fire that burns within...
Ice that clears the sin...
I need to let go of these...
That is when I'll find my peace!

Touch that melts my heart...
Whisper like the Mozart...
I know where to look for these...
It's you where I find my peace!

Dreams

Burst out, let go
Live life, a bit slow
Let me just shout and scream
Because this is what I dream...!

Laugh hard, sing loud
Forget about the silly crowd
Don't want to waste it on a ream
Because this is what I dream...!

Make time, love true
More than you could ever do
Never fall for the gleam
Because this is what I dream...!

Stay young, don't complain
Choose the uncommon lane
Join the people with a seam
Because this is what I dream...!

Get over the fears,
Get over the pains
Stop the world, from going in vain
Happy moments, are what it should seem
Isn't this what we all dream...?!

All My Life

I wish I had not been so lame
All my life, till now...
I wish I had been more understanding
All my life, till now...

Expecting the world to be crystal clear
When I myself have been so uncertain
All my life, till now...

Strangled, did I get in my emotions
Waited for someone to feel
Courage, should I have shown to my destorations
As I stood there in hope to heal
All my life, till now...

Why did I feel abandoned,
When I had so much around me
Found the world to be empty,
When it had so much to offer me
All my life, till now...

Time to break through
Time to go
For now is the phase to do so...
I will rise but not bow
For the rest of my life, starting now...!

Am I There?

When the light falls down
When it dawns the ground
I will stick to me...
Yes, I would cling to me...
But, will I be there?

When they laugh around
When the lost feels found
I will look at me...
Yes, I would heal me...
But, will I be there?

The water runs over and I'm trying to swim,
The power is over but I'm fighting to win,
They are sorry now
But I can't help...

Because I don't feel me...
Am I there?

Drowning

Love is like water
The water that rumbles
Silently, deep within

Lost of all color
More toxic, no wonder
Killing, deep within

But I can't stop jumping back inside
I need that, to breathe in time and time

I'm drowning
Under my skin, I'm counting
All the beats in my heart that are pounding
As I drown in the love of my life!

It is just another drug
That keeps me from sleeping
Silently, deep within

Not that it matters
But I'm sucked to the bottom
Killing, deep within

All the mess that is piling up and up
Now it is far beyond, to get up and give up

I'm drowning
Under my skin, I'm counting
All the beats in my heart that are pounding
As I die for the love of my life!

The Last Goodbye

The first time
When I saw you cry,
The first time
I knew it was time,

A new chapter had started
One that I waited for too long,
A new chapter uncharted
One that I needed all along,

The first time
When i made you laugh,
The first time
I knew I had passed,

A bond so pure
A friendship so innocent,
Nothing felt so secure
Nothing felt so imminent,

The first time
When I broke down,
The first time
You made it all turn around,

You made me believe
In more than myself,
You made me heal
From the world itself,

The first time
When you broke the news,
The first time
I knew I had to lose,

The day you left
The pain was too high,
But you gave me a chance
To have the last goodbye....

A New Story

I thought fairytales were real
I thought love was always in the air...
Now I have grown up and I feel
It wasn't what they said...
There is no pot of gold
There is no prince with a rose...
The older I got
The more I thought...

But then I met you
A person so alike...
You needed the same
And we just fit right...
Love feels new
With every morning kiss...
The touch of your fingers
Is more than a bliss...
Much to conquer together
But rather very young...
No happy ending yet
The story has just begun...

Stay On Board

You don't get to go
Running far away from life

Doesn't get easier
Walking up the hike

Pain is far too bold
Crashing all that it sights

It will haunt you more
Until you become the light

But you don't have to say goodbye so soon
Don't give up yet
It's all worth a try

It makes you fall
It makes you scream
It makes you question all the things you've ever
seen,
It makes you wonder
It makes you squeak
It makes you laugh at all the living silly
certainties,
Stay On Board!

Living Love

I love your lips when they are wet with mine,
And red with a wild desire...
I love your eyes when the lovelight lies,
Lit with a passionate fire...
I love your arms when the warm white flesh,
Touches mine in a fond embrace...
I love your hair when the strands enmesh,
Your kisses against my face...

So kiss me sweet with your warm wet lips,
Still fragrant with the scent of mine...
And say with a need born of a shout,
That your body and soul are mine...
Clasp me close in your warm young arms,
While the pale stars shine above...
And we will live our whole young lives away,
In the joys of a living love...!

She

She makes mistakes
But she tries

She loves too hard
She loves too well

She knows still
She'll be broken at the end

She cannot see
The beauty within

She tries all well
To be perfect and clean

She has lost too much
But will not show

She knows the world cares less
For all her woes

Sometimes she wishes
To end it all

But she just lets it out
And then builds a wall

She won't change herself
Cannot fall down

She will remain different
From the world around…

Overthinking

I know the pain it brings
I know the joy it kills
I still can't let it go

My friends call me out
But I have too much doubt
All my pursuits before the start
End within my mind and heart

It pulls me far
It pulls me within
And shows me the horror
As I hide it all in

Now I am toxic
Now I am the evil
The darkness summons
More powerful and lethal…

A Mockingbird

As I stroll down the path
Of an enchanted land,
I look up-to the trees
And closer do I stand,
A gush of euphoria
As I feel within,
I hum a melody
And I start to sing,
A faint whisper afar
Or rather a song,
I look all around
And follow it along,
High up in the sky
Rests a creature so serene,
Its voice so pure
It makes me heal,
A mockingbird sits
In a world so quiet,
It mocks my song
Its eyes remain unbiased,
I smile with peace
It fills my heart,
To know a mockingbird saw
Within me, a spark…

Don't Give Up

You can fall down
You can cry all about
But you can't give up…

You can make a mess
You can wish for the best
But you can't give up…

You can hate the world
Or live it with fear
But you can't give up…

You can tumble afar
You can kill your spark
But you can't give up…

You can heal yourself
You can be the power itself
Then you won't give up…!

A Simple Life

A simple word
A simpler meaning
Now filled with chaos
Beyond any winning…

A simple moment
A simpler feeling
But it hurts so much
When nothing is healing

A simple laugh
A simpler reason
It changes a lot
With the changing season…

A simple wish
A simpler prayer
But it it breaks
There is no repair…

A simple life
A simpler living
It comes by hard
But is more than giving…